# Only A Dream

DON T RESIO

Copyright © 2019 by Don T Resio.

ISBN Softcover    978-1-950580-57-6

All rights reserved. No part of this book may be reproduced or transmitted in any form or by any means, electronic or mechanical, including photocopying, recording, or by any information storage and retrieval system without express written permission from the author, except in the case of brief quotations embodied in critical reviews and certain other non-commercial uses permitted by copyright law.

Printed in the United States of America.

To order additional copies of this book, contact:
**Bookwhip**
1-855-339-3589
https://www.bookwhip.com

# Contents

Prologue to a Dream ................................................................. vii

## THE DREAM BEGINS . . .

A Midsummer Night ................................................................. 3
Soliloquy at a Funeral ............................................................... 4
Reprise to a Soliloquy ............................................................... 6

## SOFTLY THE SEASONS . . .

Seasons ................................................................................... 9
Rain ...................................................................................... 12
The Dome of Crystal Blue ...................................................... 14
On the Autumn Ground ........................................................ 17
Time and a Tree .................................................................... 19
Paths .................................................................................... 22
Time ..................................................................................... 23
A Toast to Time (Variation on a Theme) ................................ 23

## A WORLD WITHIN A WORLD . . .

A Country Road .................................................................... 27
Fredericksburg ...................................................................... 28
The Southern Front .............................................................. 30
Vicksburg—1219 Adams Street ............................................. 32
Vicksburg Battlefield—Early July .......................................... 34
Warehouse, Circa 1925 ......................................................... 35
City Jazz ............................................................................... 37
This City's Circus Tent .......................................................... 38
A Solitary House On a Snow-Covered Hill ............................. 39
The Lake ............................................................................... 40
Seven Steps .......................................................................... 42
Night Storm ......................................................................... 46

## WITHIN MY DREAMS—DARK AND LIGHT . . .

Midnight Reverie ........................................................................... 49
Fallen Angels................................................................................. 51
Fallen Angel—San Antonio .......................................................... 52
Dark City Blues............................................................................. 53
Night Shadow ............................................................................... 55
Don T's Inferno ............................................................................ 57
Nighttime Labyrinth..................................................................... 58
The Huntress ................................................................................ 62
The Other Side ............................................................................. 63
Two Candles ................................................................................. 65

## THE SEA INSIDE ME . . .

Envy .............................................................................................. 69
The Sea Within Me ...................................................................... 70
Voices in the Sea 1 ........................................................................ 71
Voices in the Sea 2 ........................................................................ 72
Caribbean Jewels........................................................................... 73
Colors of the Sea: Morning .......................................................... 75
Sea of Sand.................................................................................... 77
On a Windward Beach.................................................................. 78

## THE SOUND OF ONE MAN LAUGHING . . .

I Fear Nothing .............................................................................. 81
Amid a Million Masks................................................................... 82
The Fairie World .......................................................................... 83
Tonight, Tonight Or Not.............................................................. 85
Teenage Madness .......................................................................... 86
Greed ............................................................................................ 87
Tequila Wasteland......................................................................... 89
If Truth Were a River .................................................................. 91
Southern Tea................................................................................. 92
The Dove and the Pigeon ............................................................. 94
Meandering................................................................................... 95

Epilogue: Dreams Never End........................................................ 97

# Prologue to a Dream

*. . . Come*
*Walk with me through this dream of mine*
*Over paths untrodden and intertwined*
*Through time and space within my mind*
*Linger here with me until you find*
*That place you thought you'd left behind*
*But no maps here, roads neatly lined*
*Can lead you where you want to go*

*Slip away with me from daylit skies*
*Let dreams descend upon your eyes*
*And each moment form a new surprise*
*Put there by muses in disguise*
*From earthbound light and the moon's soft shine*
*They could become tales of such grand design*
*If we'd only let them grow*

*On roads unmarked with twists and bends*
*Passing through worlds and worlds again*
*As one story ends another begins*
*No rush to finish no race to win*
*The dream moves on and never ends*

# The Dream Begins . . .

# A Midsummer Night

*To Ron—To know him is to know his dreams*

*To be young again in summer*
*Lying upon the wet evening grass*
*Watching countless stars twinkle above*
*While a warm summer wind brushes*
*Gently by your face.*

*To talk of young ideas*
*With a brother forever young*
*Weaving a sense of wonder*
*With a life now just begun*

*To walk through this summer's night*
*Holding it so very tight*
*That you can feel it pressed*
*Against your soul.*

*The ebb and flow of yesterdays*
*That you know will never die.*
*While watching webs of golden light*
*Being woven in the sky.*

*Such a sweet, tender night . . .*
*Every dream still lay ahead . . .*
*No path before us dead.*
*Can you remember still that night*
*As slowly fades your life's last light?*
*If you can then surely, Ron.*
*There shall come for you another dawn;*
*And you shall never pass this way;*
*But will embrace each newborn day*
*Beyond your summer's night.*

# Soliloquy at a Funeral

*Ron is dead*
*So much to be said*
*But the words stay trapped inside my head*
*We shared a bond*
*By death unbroken*
*Our voices now bound by words not spoken*

*Tears being shed*
*Not just by me*
*But by all around that I can see*
*I should speak*
*I try to begin*
*But all my words are drowned within*
*Within my soul within the air*
*I still see him standing there*

*How can I speak*
*Within this room*
*Within this passage to his tomb?*
*We used to talk of how we felt*
*When outside feelings screamed inside us*
*Now I am trapped in such a place*
*And nowhere within for me to hide us*

*I cannot speak*
*However short, however brief*
*I can only feel our pain—our grief*
*I cannot say what should be said*
*I only sit and bow my head.*
*Somewhere my own voice is oh so ready*
*To sing his praise in words so steady*
*To talk of times when he was young*

*And how we two were really one*
*To tell them of just what it means*
*To know someone with such dreams*
*To bring him back for all to see*
*One last time for all to see . . .*
*But somehow my soliloquy*
*Can't find the strength to tear me free*
*From his voice still there inside my head*
*But . . . Ron is dead.*

# Reprise to a Soliloquy

But with his death he left his voice
And now I know I have no choice
But to write these dreams he could not live
Not for the soliloquy I could not give
But so part of him lives on

# Softly the Seasons . . .

# Seasons

Winter's white hair falls carelessly cross
Pale grey hills 'neath a silvery sky.
No one to mourn this Winter's loss
As she lies silent, waiting to die.
The snow disappears
Just cold winter tears
Which feed the birth of Spring.

Newborn Spring, dressed in downy green,
Toddles barefoot over paths unseen
Musical laughter shimmers in the air
While playful young breezes tug on her hair.
The gentle sound of a stream passing through
An early morning valley with jewels of dew.
Whispers of time now just begun
Of life filled forever with games and with fun.

But a time such as this can never stand still.
Like a mountain stream touched by winter's chill
It changes before us while seeming the same;
And even though the girl still plays at her game
And is not yet ready to move on
Spring is gone.


One by one . . . fireflies bring Summer from
Some place where Summer must always live on.
Nightly offerings of light add to the sun;
Forming golden beams of purest gold spun
That dance over fields each new day begun;
And Summer is roused by the song being sung.

*Warm winds blow on this moist, hot dawn*
*And childhood is lost in the feelings they spawn.*
*Young heat fed by Summer, soon to be fires,*
*New feelings emerge, new thoughts and desires.*
*The heat from within forges feelings so strong,*
*Bare bodies merging as they try to belong*
*To the summer heat that haunts their days*
*And the sultry dance that beckons and sways*
*Moving, moving and then grasping so tight,*
*Through both faces of Summer . . . first day and then night.*

*It seems it should last forever again*
*And again and again and again and again.*
*But time is fickle and cannot stand still*
*And one firefly leaves and another until*
*They have taken Summer and left in its wake*
*A crisp Autumn morning over a clear mountain lake.*
*Early fall calls*
*Like nightfall*
*While fires all*
*Are damped to hold on to Summer's flame.*
*And for a while the embers yet burn*
*And for a while the days yet turn*
*Orange and bright*
*But every night*
*The moon grows larger—feeding on the earth's last heat.*

*Memories of warmth color our dreams.*
*And fires from the past warm our days.*
*Shadows and light mix in pale moonbeams*
    *A strange coolness in these rays.*

*Then Winter must come, and come it soon will*
*Early snows soon cover each valley and hill*
*Trees shed their leaves until now there are none*
*While cold wooden voices beg alms from the sun*
*Stark branches all shiver the same gnarled way*
*Trying their best to keep Winter at bay*

*When all heat is fled*
*Winter calls to the dead*
*And spirits sing in the wind,*
*A windswept song that Winter sends*
*To call us all home again.*

*Winter's white hair falls carelessly cross*
*Pale grey hills 'neath a cold grey sky.*
*There's no one to mourn for winter's loss*
*As she lies silent, waiting to die.*


*Postscript . . .*

*Why can't we learn from these cycles unending*
*And tear down these useless walls we're defending?*
*You'd think that after we've seen loved ones die*
*We'd stop and think and question why.*
*Why do we fill our lives with time spent chasing?*
*Why waste them with worry and senseless racing . . .*
*To and fro, to and fro*
*How much faster can we go?*

# Rain

Past my window wet silver streaks
Join others down below
Framed within the waning light
Trees dance rhythms to and fro.

Translucent curtains
Close around me
As the rain forms
A diffuse boundary
That draws me inward

On the window a wet spiderweb
Forms as droplets slowly flow and ebb
Pausing then trickling, shimmering down
Watery tracks without a sound.
Small streams slipping
Into droplets dripping . . .
Constantly changing
And rearranging
Patterns before my eyes.

Reflected there in the windowpane
In half-mirrored light a face appears
It seems to float inside the rain
Or perhaps just somewhere very near.
Is it me? I wonder now
If it is, I wonder how
Inside I stay so dry.

*There is a feeling that I feel*
*In the softness of this day*
*A fleeting feeling more than real*
*That keeps the world at bay*
*The rain wraps close about me*
*It's forever 'til tomorrow*
*I feel spirits now surround me*
*In time here only borrowed*
*Leading to a place where*
*. . . I find the time*
*To savor slowly*
*Like well-aged wine*
*The rain*

# The Dome of Crystal Blue

Autumn's last tears—now just icy-cold fingers
Hang in silence from the limbs of a tree.
Yet within this cold sky the spirit still lingers
Of times past and those yet to be.

Nearby, a cabin at this end of the earth
With a solitary small girl at its window
A fire gives warmth from an old stone hearth
Its roots set in times long ago.
As cold as death, the world outside;
As warm as life, the world within.

A lone sparrow, abandoned in the sky,
Draws frigid circles in the wind.
Tired and near frozen, the warmth of summer
Fading to only a spark within.
Black, black eyes, life's light only a glimmer;
Sad, searching eyes growing dimmer and dimmer.
His flight . . . lower and still lower
His motions . . . slower and still slower.

Watched by sad gentle eyes
The bird lands on a limb,
Against winter blue skies
Just a shadow in the wind.
A tear runs down the girl's soft young cheek
A last strangled cry flies from the bird's beak.
And with that cry all hope flies too
And under that dome of crystal blue
The bird falls into the snow.

*For a moment all is still*
*For an eternity . . . time is frozen*
*From somewhere within this small girl's will*
*A cry breaks free and time flows on*
*Dashing out the door in only bare feet*
*Into the heart of winter's quiet calling.*
*No thought of what fate she might meet*
*Salty tears become snowflakes falling.*

*Straining against winter's icy grip*
*She lunges forward trying not to slip*
*For she knows the cold of this winter snow*
*Would trap her soul and never let go.*
*There's the tree now not so far ahead.*
*She closes her eyes and prays it's not dead.*
*Finally, she comes to a hole in the snow*
*And pushes in her hand ever so slow*
*Into an icy-white crypt.*

*Lifting the bird gently in a trembling hand*
*She feels only the stark stillness of this winter land*
*No sign of life, no spark, no light.*
*She pulls it near and holds it tight*
*Shivering she slides it inside her shirt.*
*Please, please just for once,*
*Let her warm tears wash away this hurt.*

*But, no life grows in the warmth she shares.*
*No answer comes to her wordless prayers.*
*And now the cold, gnawing on her bare feet*
*Climbs up her body, stealing its heat*
*A dull fear fills her when she sees her home*
*So far away under this crystal blue dome*
*But her will is the strong will of those still young.*
*So, step by step back the path she'd come*
*Dreams of warmth flutter in her heart still breaking.*
*Yet the cold cuts deeper with each step she's taking.*

Each step is slower and still slower
Her body . . . sinks lower and still lower.
She falls onto her back and stares into the sky
Her hopes and her dreams fly away with a sigh
Still hugging her bird so close to her chest
Her hair fallen forward into a soft nest . . .

But where once was only one, now there are two
Lives looking up at the sky so blue
The bird stirs and moving wakes the child
She sits and senses life still coursing wild
Between her and the bird and the tree.
She sees renewed promise through a door open wide
Now only a few short steps from her side.
Then the bird and she hurry past
The grasp of winter and are home at last.

Through a frost-covered window, it seems to them
That they can see Spring's first virgin stem
Peeking up through the ice and snow.
Within the warm cabin, within its warm glow
Their lives no longer seem Winter's to take
They feel its cold grip beginning to break,
Each life alone could never stand
Under this sky in this bleak land.
But somehow when their souls were joined
And not just one and one apart
No longer could their lives be taken
By the icy cold of Winter's heart.

But then they heard an eerie windy voice
Your lives have been spared but by my choice
You, child, have a sense of wonder.
Warm spring rains and summer thunder
Will share your love of life so clearly shown
When to save the bird you risked your own.
So, life's child, I want you to know
I had you both and let you go.

# *On the Autumn Ground*

Memories of Summer drive him on
But within the sounds of Autumn's song
The deep blue sky tells him Winter's near
Though its frozen winds are not yet here
He traces a path only he can see
Amid a swirl of leaves set free
From last Summer's green on a Summer tree,
Now dancing to Fall's last symphony
Singing
Of winds that paint the air
Of rains that cool the earth
Of clouds that even dare
To watch the nightly birth
Of specters on the Autumn ground.

The sun has lost its Summer flame
To Autumn winds that call his name.
And the bright heat of Summer's skies
Darken now with dim goodbyes.
Along this path within his mind
The trees and vines all close behind
Him as he passes along this way
Searching, searching through his day . . .
For something on the Autumn Ground.

Then night has come and day is gone
Yet still he hears the Autumn song
Within these woods within this night
Along pale-lit paths of soft moonlight
Autumn's dance is everywhere
Within the moonlit-speckled air
In breezes brushing through his hair
And within his softly whispered prayer
Falling silently to the Autumn ground
Then . . .

*He feels the warmth of life within
Of all that was and still is in him.
Out of his past, out of his dream
Before him sits the Autumn Queen.
She laughs and smiles a smile
That makes him feel again a child.
And he remembers—*

*County fairs on a frosty night
Cotton candy clouds in day's last light
The first time ever he held a girl tight—
Their own warmth burning through the night.
The touch of cold air on an Autumn morn
And the color of fall in rows of corn
And on and on and on and on
Silently flow the scenes of Fall.
From times long past he remembers all—
A voice that told him once of such things
As soaring geese on sky-framed wings
And windowpanes painted white by frost
And where to look for things he'd lost
There on the Autumn ground.*

*For an eternity the two are one
As she sings of times just now begun
Of all the mysteries in the earth
The sadness of death and beauty of birth.
And he feels her soul reach out to him
To give him peace and rest within;
And to let him know he's found his way
Past a timeless door and now can stay
Forever here on the Autumn ground.*

*Walking away and glancing behind
A song fades slowly within his mind
He sees a glimmer within the air
Hovering o'er someone lying there
    On the Autumn Ground.*

# *Time and a Tree*

Rough arms thrusting toward the sun
On a day when springtime's new warmth
Is worn like a cloak
By limbs long too cold through the winter.
A solitary tree stands here,
Rooted firmly on this barren hill.
Perhaps it had been forever that this tree
Had stood upon this craggy spot . . . or not;
Perhaps it was just since a long yesterday,
A single long night . . .
Followed by the timid strands of one new day.
The tree did not know.

However long the time, it knew
One thing had been forever true.
It had stood alone until this spring
And never once had one living thing
Come near.

The tree was content to stand this way . . .
Until the day
A solitary song broke through the mist
From a random somewhere far away.
The song shimmered in sharpened hues
The tree never heard before.

And the tree silently pleaded
To hear again that sound
Still filling his world
With new feelings found.

Then, winging through the light
A single bird in flight
Unbound and flying free . . .
And flying toward the tree.

*For another life to come so near*
*Sent senses strangely tingling*
*Through his wooden veins.*
*Then a second bird came into sight*
*Answering the song still ringing*
*Through his deeply rooted chains.*

*All spring the birds stayed with him,*
*From his twigs they built a nest.*
*His heart at first so old so cold*
*Soon felt warmth grow in his chest*

*He heard them talk of love*
*He heard them talk of pain*
*He watched them flying free*
*Always to return again.*

*He learned so much that Spring*
*As the sun rose through the sky.*
*He carefully sheltered all the young*
*Until they too could learn to fly.*
*And in the Summer's dusty heat*
*He cooled them with his shade.*
*He felt their life spread through him*
*From the nestled home they made.*

*They taught the young ones love*
*They warned them of the pain*
*They set them free to fly*
*Knowing they'd return again.*

*But then there came the Autumn*
*As Autumns always will.*
*The birds still sang their summer songs*
*To ward away its chill.*
*But the sun did not hear their call;*
*And one morning waking late that Fall,*
*With the sun so low*
*They had to go.*

*They sang to him tales of love*
*And warned him of the pain*
*Then they flew away together*
*And did not return again.*

*The tree forgot their warning*
*And deep within his sorrow.*
*He yearned for his yesterday*
*And feared his long tomorrow.*

*He wanted to follow*
*He wanted to fly*
*He wanted no roots*
*He wanted to die.*
*He had given his soul and only asked*
*Them to stay.*
*Why had they come into his world*
*On that bright, hateful day.*
*Was it better to have never known this life*
*Than to feel such pain and loss?*
*Could he go back to what he was before . . .*
*Within the lifeless frost?*

*Yet somehow within the winter wind*
*A song still echoed from last Spring.*
*He had lost his sense of timelessness*
*And was unsure what fate might bring.*
*He felt his heart starting to harden*
*Blindly he cursed the choice he chose;*
*Yet somehow, their song still lingered*
*And in the Spring—who knows.*

# *Paths*

Winter's icy breath laces the trees
Under moon-painted phantoms racing clouds.
A touch of snow sparkles the breeze
Adding texture to winter's white shrouds.
Then, all sounds cease—the forest waits.
A single leaf struggles, then loses its grip,
Falling fearfully into an unknown fate,
The Winter wind captures this storm-tossed ship.

Riding turbulent currents whimsically swirled
Past sharp wooden limbs with fingers curled
It sails into the night
Over streams hard frozen
Toward a field now chosen
To end its short-lived flight.

But just a blink before landing there,
Another path for this leaf appears
And one last gust lofts it high in the air
Past the dark night with all its fears
Fate has carefully chosen a new resting place
As a bright splash of gold ends its ride
Against a window . . . and a little girl's face,
Is startled to laughter with eyes open wide.

A child who knows no world so vast
As this leaf touched by summer's past
That came just once to pass this way,
Along one of many paths that day.

# Time

Time speaks so softly
We often don't hear
The passing of days
Of months—of years.
But when it speaks loudly
We can't ignore
The changes from who
We were before.

# A Toast to Time
### (Variation on a Theme)

Time speaks so softly
We often don't hear
The days passing by—
The months—the years.
But at times like this
We can't ignore
The changes from who
We were before

So I offer a toast
To those of us here
May time's pace be slow
And friends always be near
May we finish what we start
And start more every day
And may we always give more
Than we take away.

*A World Within a World . . .*

# *A Country Road*

A country road, running through some hills,
Its past almost hidden from sight,
Moving slowly along a winding path,
In soft shades of shadowed light
Cast by the late-day sun.

Pieces of cabins by the side of the road
Mark places where families once grew;
Pieces of lives still can be found
In the remnants of rooms they once knew
As Home.

Along this road — a door to the past lies open.
Lit by timeless starry nights
Still shedding meteoritic tears upon us
For all the could haves and maybes and mights
That died within our dreams
    Country dreams of love and laughter
    And family ties hang from each rafter
    Along this country road.

# Fredericksburg

*Solemn buildings watch a silent street
On this cold and wintry night
Their memories from times long ago
Rise up to fill my sight.
Scenes of peace, scenes of war,
Held by chains bound ever tight
Play nightly on a silent stage
Within the soft lamplight*

*Time runs strong within this street . . .
And each cobble here has been
Washed by countless tears,
Imprisoned by nameless fears,
Cut deep by senseless hate,
And cursed by mindless fate.*

*But these same stones
Have also felt the spark of life
Within each child at play
Felt passion in each man and wife
Still sleepless at the break of day.
And each has heard the jubilant song
Raised by lives that still belong
Within this street.*

*Tonight, peering out from behind a cloud,
Is the same moon that once did shine
Upon this street when it was young.
Yet, tonight its light seems only mine
As I stand here down below.*

*I see, framed against these gypsy clouds,*
*Church spires still pointing to the sky.*
*Silent sentinels that have watched in faith*
*As each newborn hope learned to fly*
*And rise above this street.*

*Tonight the past is painted here*
*By winter's winds with subdued light.*
*And bright swirls of Monet colors*
*Become just shades of black and white.*
*Translucent spirits now rise from the street.*
*Meeting snowflakes newly falling.*
*And the gentle touch of some former life*
*Is like an urgent lover calling*
*Me back to her bed so soft,*
*Past doors and windows laced with frost*
*Into a world of new hopes and dreams*
*And rainbows cast by prismed beams.*
*Then . . . I feel the brush of restless souls*
*As slowly a midnight church bell tolls,*
*A fading patter of running feet*
*Then all is still within the street.*

# *The Southern Front*

For over a day the grey marches forth
Aroused and rising—its forces push north
Humidity is nurtured in warm soaked air
And grey cloaks soon hang everywhere
In a sky so thick you can almost swim in it

Sporadic skirmishes soon send rain below
And the forces of grey continue to grow
Nothing can stop this relentless attack
Yet to the north blue forces start to push back
And the winds of war begin to blow

And as lightning dances storm to storm
A peaceful truce is shattered then torn
Thundering cannons again fill the skies
Reenacting past battles long before sunrise
Can even let us see our foe

Northern forces push southward from far away
While ominous clouds still hold back the day
Winds rage together all twisted and twirled
Carving paths of destruction deep into our world
That live on within our minds

Wild winds now scream a savage rebel yell
The thunder rolls toward us—shell after shell
But the grey forces—though starting to wane
Still charge blindly into pouring rain
Forming clay red streams on this land

*Inch by inch driven by forces of blue*
*The morning light now almost shines through*
*And grey clouds surrender in sad retreat*
*Though never, never admitting defeat*
*As they pass out of sight*

*So now at the end of this heated attack*
*With the grey ever so slowly driven back*
*I sense that somewhere deep within*
*This land of bibles and hidden sin*
*The grey will always rise again*

# Vicksburg—1219 Adams Street

*It was spring and outside the rain*
*Became long lines of silver*
*Through a wet emerald twilight*
    *Soft-edged shadows crept*
*Across the walls, reaching*
    *Toward the coming night*
*It was then she saw him*
*Standing there*
*A pale apparition*
*Within the air*
*Faintly formed in tattered grey*
*A young man watched the dying day*

*In this light the sad-faced*
*Youth seemed but a shadow*
    *Within the evening haze*
*It seemed at first that this*
*Must be a trick such as*
    *Twilight sometimes plays.*
*But as she moved closer*
*The specter slowly turned*
*And she saw within his eyes*
*A restless fire that burned*
*Hot, still raging within his soul*
*And as distant thunder began to roll*
*He began to tell his tale—*

*I have seen loved ones die*
*That should be living still*
*Mothers and children and men alike*
*Struck down upon this hill*
*Days and nights just like today*
*Filled with the scent of fear*
*And time standing oh so still when*

The sounds of war drew near
Storms like tonight still wake me
And I try hard to understand
Why we suffered so much together
Trying only to defend our land;

Yet after we had starved for weeks
And had given no matter what it cost
Had given and given 'til all was gone
Somehow we still had lost.
So, there are no great tales of deeds
About how we saved our town;
And after all we'd been through
We watched our flag torn down.
Now I wander on nights like this
When I hear thunder begin to roar
And search my soul for an answer
Could we have given more?
So, no heroes or heroines are buried here
And time cannot ease my soul's distress
Is it that our tears were less sincere
Or that we somehow loved the less . . .

Then he looked to see if she could find
Some words to give him peace of mind;
But there were no words that she could say
To turn his night back into day
So as the thunder rolled again
The specter's eyes met hers and then
He vanished into the night.

# Vicksburg Battlefield–Early July

Roads lined with monuments . . .

Built on memories of blood and fear
Left by both armies fallen here,
Scars still haunt this battlefield
That all the years still have not healed.

This morning . . .

Insects still drone a last Post and Chorus
To men, brave and scared, who died here before us.
And slowing my pace and closing my eyes
I hear fragments of voices as I pass by.
They whisper of lives too soon left behind
And lives that should still lie ahead,
A lingering cry for some peace of mind
From these dreams that haunt the dead,
Sleeping here in this warm field
Weeping here in this warm field
For scars that have not healed
These scars set deep inside us
That somehow still divide us

# Warehouse, Circa 1925

*An old building,*
*Tattered walls*
*Beside a road.*
*Time paused here*
*Then passed by.*

*Why does it*
*Call to me?*
*What is my*
*Bond to this past?*

*I feel the*
*Lives that lived here.*
*More so than if they*
*Still lived today.*

*Somehow time has*
*Kept this feeling*
*Here for someone*
*Someone perhaps like me.*

*Did once a young man*
*Build his dreams here*
*Perhaps if I look*
*I will still find*
*Part of his soul*
*Within these walls.*

*Perhaps his young wife*
*Brought him lunch*
*And on hot days*
*They ate in the shade*
*Of that old tree.*

*Whatever happened here*
*Has left its mark.*
*And will not be forgotten*
*As long as these tattered walls*
*Live on.*

# *City Jazz*

*No sky looks down on the city tonight,*
*Just a dingy ceiling of dark city light.*
*A damp cool mist soon fills the street*
*Marking the passage of tired wet feet*
*That weave in and out of buildings built*
*Upon the pages of these lives.*

*A low moan whispers into my ear*
*So low at first I cannot hear*
*The words trapped there within.*
*Amid this jumble*
*Subways rumble*
*Junkies stumble*
*And hustlers mumble*
*Meaningless sounds into the din.*

*There is a sound I strain to hear*
*Beneath the car horns all too clear*
*Voices left by those who walked this way*
*Night by night and day by day*
*Uptown bleakness quietly sighing*
*Lower side sadness hopelessly crying*
*Caught in this sound that traps their souls;*
*Spending their time—playing their roles*
*Within each nighttime scene.*

*Working women looking so fine*
*Street people with their breaths of wine.*
*Preachers sinning and sinners preaching*
*Shrill voices blending with tires still screeching*
*Some couples together and some still not and*
*Singles playing parts too soon forgotten*
*But oh so real tonight.*

*Within the city a chorus builds*
*From age to age and name to name*
*A different song for each of us*
*Yet somehow still the same . . .*

# This City's Circus Tent

Midnight shadows fly ever higher
First only embers then turning to fires
As though within these funeral pyres
They become whatever they aspire
To be within the city's glow
And all these dazzling bright reflections
Blur the rough-cut imperfections
Of those living down below

So high above the city streets
Muffled sounds—just throbbing beats
Are felt deep within our souls
And in this sky these lights arrayed
As though predestined where each is laid
To echo these earthbound tolls

From here the lights are clean and bright
Above the subways of the night
Where lives below are spent
A carnival of lights and heights
Built upon dreams and spotlight beams
In this city's circus tent.

# A Solitary House
# On a Snow-Covered Hill

A solitary house on a snow-covered hill
Sounds muffled by the midwinter chill
A full moon sails high above the sky
Through midnight blue and indigo dye
Leaving a luminous wake of golden light
Spirals and swirls that dance in the night
A moon's so jealous it will not share
The sky with stars that are not there
And so tonight's alone

No lights through the windows show
No footprints in the cold night snow
But there within these walls I know
Fireplace embers still faintly glow
Drawing long shadows on the floor
Flickering up walls and on each door
Feeling the warmth those living here
And all the life that I sense so near
That makes this house a home

A strange magic is here tonight
Within this world of winter delight
And beneath the grudging moon's bitter glow
The house sleeps sweetly in its blanket of snow.
A blanket that covers all in sight
With the softest fabric of woven white
And no one can ever pass this way
Without hearing the promise of the coming day
That resonates within

# *The Lake*

*(dedicated to Mary Lynn and Eureka Springs)*

A bleak winter sky over a grey-blue lake
The seed of winter a single, small snowflake,
I gaze at the surface and at first I see
A blurred, imperfect skyline, a hill, a tree.
It seems that ripples, waves, and such
Distort and cover so very much
Of what I see in the world above.

But then I look still deeper . . .

And, there appears before my eyes,
Not just a reflection of pale winter skies
A world is formed, that is much, much more
And the lake's surface is but a door
Into this other world.

There, among the eddies and whirls
A world full of wonder before me unfurls.
The winter sky above so still, forlorn
But there below, earth's magic lives on.
Sea serpents sailing through watery nights
Sandcastles built by mischievous sprites
All from our world above have fled.
But here below they are not dead.

*I sense a power in this magic land*
*That lies between the waves and sand.*
*And realize that what I first saw as less*
*I must confess*
*Was only less in me.*

*Though time here did pause briefly for me*
*It can never truly set you free;*
*And I slowly begin to realize*
*I must return to my winter skies.*
*I caught a glimpse from where I stand*
*Of a world I cannot enter . . . and*
*Although my mind still wants to stay*
*I cannot shut out the winter day.*
*So, it seems it must be my fate*
*To live where life can only imitate*
  *. . . the lake.*

# Seven Steps

Seven steps climbed up to a porch
Lit there by a single torch.
I heard him call in tones so low
I almost didn't stop or slow
But then I saw his rheumy eyes
Pleading that I would recognize
The person still within

A ragged scarecrow of a man
Slowly raised a tattered arm
And pulled me into his world

From this man now almost dead
I was captured by a single thread
What if it were I instead
Who called to those who quickly tread
By and did not stay

I saw him shudder and stagger down
One step below without a sound
Then I heard his voice now stronger
And saw within his eyes no longer
The fear that had been there before

Even his clothes seemed different now
And nodding his head in a silent bow
As though he stood but on a stage
Waiting for me to turn the page
To send him on his way.

The stiffness of someone very old
Strained to move within the cold
And the damp night air unnaturally still
Wrapped him in its bitter chill
But he managed one more step.

*Now my eyes were opened wide*
*Night's cold fingers touched deep inside*
*He seemed to change and change until*
*He stood before me much younger still*
*Than I knew I'd seen before.*

*Raising his head he breathed in slow*
*Now younger even than me below*
*He seemed no longer ready*
*To breathe his last breath*
*His gaze was now steady*
*Not tainted with death*

*As he took his next step I heard a deep sigh*
*As a much younger spirit was now set free*
*Reflecting the torchlight into my eye*
*A vision of who he might be*

*One more step and I saw standing there*
*A mere teenage boy with sandy red hair*
*He paused now to savor each feeling*
*The first time love sent his heart reeling*
*And long days that warmed him*
*And longer nights that charmed him*

*But as I watched he looked into the night*
*At something far beyond my sight*
*As though he knew he could not stay*
*On his long passage home today*
*He took another step.*

*Now a child of seven or eight*
*Laughed out loud but didn't wait*
*Before I could say no*
*He stepped below*
*And was only two or three*

*One more step to the cold ground*
*If those small bare feet moved again*
*One last step to be all the way down*
*What would happen then?*

*Slowly,*
*The little child with eyes so, so bright*
*They burned the fabric of the night*
*Smiled a smile not of a child*
*But of something older, something wild*
*That lived outside the day*

*I knew I was lost*
*Feet anchored in frost*
*I was far too cold*
*And much too old*
*To run away*

*Somehow . . .*
*I forced my eyes to focus and*
*Within this child still stood the man*
*That I'd first seen on the seventh stair*
*The same wizened spirit was still there*
*Inside those night-bright eyes*

*Captured by his burning stare*
*Sparks spewed brightly into the air*
*Each carried an image that swirled around*
*Before falling silent to the ground*
*And as each one passed it told a story*
*Of how the man came from this boy*

*As the last light*
*Fled the night*
*I rubbed my eyes and looking down*
*Before me now just eyes of brown*
*But as I reached to touch his face*

*He disappeared without a trace*
*Within my head within my mind*
*I searched for what I couldn't find*

*Then on the seventh step*
*A ragged scarecrow of a man*
*Slowly lowered a tattered arm*
*And released me from his world*

*Within the dusk*
*A hollow husk*
*Is all that now remains*
*And the cold night*
*That bound him tight*
*Releases him from his chains*

*Slowly he fades*
*To formless shades*
*Now just a misty blur*
*An open door*
*Is closed once more*
*And the night begins to stir*

*Night sounds now rejoin the air*
*I sense that he's no longer there*
*But a thin voice rasps inside my head*
*You could have passed but you instead*
*Looked past my aged skin*
*To the life I once had within*
*The final act for me has come*
*Nothing's left that's still undone*

# Night Storm

The sky flashes jagged in jigsaw pieces
Lightning blazing along the creases
A wild wind pouncing from tree to tree
Chases invisible beasts that try to flee
Before it

Lost souls hunted by the devil's own hounds
There's no escaping these hell-spawned sounds
Of breaking, crashing
Grinding and gnashing
Of teeth

Within the raw fury now piercing the night
Light burns dark and dark burns with light
And thunder growls
And the wind howls
At the earth

Lightning-burnt script—unnaturally bright
Leaves permanent scars within this night
A tattoo writ inside my mind
From an older yet younger time
In my life

# Within My Dreams— Dark and Light . . .

# *Midnight Reverie*

A midnight song sings to my soul
As dreamlit light surrounds me
A hazy sound within my mind
No rhyme or meter or key

Like the patter of rain in staccato time
Notes landing drop by drop
I dare not move nor even breathe
Please don't let it stop

Time is stilled within this song
Tomorrow's not a choice
This plaintive sound within my head
Seduces me with her voice

A gentle tug—I'm pulled along
Outside myself inside the song
Now swept by a growing tide
Feelings erupt and grow inside

She sings of times forgotten
And loved ones now long dead
She sings of life still vibrant
Beside me in my bed

She sings of greenest valleys
Of spirits in the night
She sings of children playing
In moments like tonight

*I lose myself within this night*
*Far better than a dream*
*I feel my mind reach out to her*
*But it tears a fragile seam*

*Her voice first just softens*
*Then slowly fades away*
*In the cold, cold night*
*Why couldn't she stay?*

# Fallen Angels

*Fallen Angels . . .*
*Standing in the halo of a pale street light,*
*Watching the world through painted eyes,*
*In lives custom fit to the dark of night*
*From the edge of dusk to the next sunrise*

*Calling out promises to passing cars,*
*Like Today's painted Sirens under sequined stars*
*Tonight they stalk like wolves for prey*
*Beckoning each soul to stop and play*

*What birthplace calls these angels home?*
*What childhood dreams still haunt their day?*
*What led them to these streets alone*
*And left their dreams so far away?*

*What happened in these lives to change them so?*
*Was it a slow maze turning round and round?*
*Or did they pass into night's neon glow*
*Through a single door without a sound?*

# Fallen Angel–San Antonio

*A Fairy Princess when she was young*
*Her laughter lit the skies*
*And each night when the moon was hung*
*It was only for her eyes.*
*For her, the sun rose bright and fair*
*Gently waking each spring flower*
*While her tiny feet on invisible stairs*
*Carried her up the magic tower*
*And to her throne came butterflies*
*With nectar for her days*
*And hummingbirds with honey pies*
*On tiny golden trays.*
*And if she turned her head just right*
*She could feel her magic grow*
*And there in the soft hued fairy light*
*The whole world lay below.*
*When she was young she traveled wide*
*In search of Fairy Gold*
*With elves and fairies by her side*
*She never could grow old.*

*But,*
*Today I saw her on the street*
*Matted hair and dirty bare feet*
*In the midday sun she lay asleep*
*Dreaming dreams she could not keep*
*When she wakes into this day.*

*This teenaged girl all tattered and torn*
*On a city street all battered and worn.*
*Is there a princess still held tight*
*Within her dreams, within her night?*
*And in her days where dreams can't hide*
*Can dreams like hers live on inside?*

# Dark City Blues

*Time in nature is carved in stone*
*But a city's soul is steel and bone*
*Lives spent here in hopeless trouble*
*Bound by chains within the rubble*
*No pretty sounds*
*Just city sounds*
*Filling all the streets*

*Burned out lives, windows boarded*
*Anything good is elsewhere hoarded*
*Gutted houses, news at ten*
*Same thing tomorrow all over again*
*Worn-out lives in bodies worn down*
*Dark city blues keep coming around*
*Playing day and night*

*City children stare with eyes of ice*
*You negotiate—they pay the price*
*With so little hope for a better life*
*Souls are bought by a gun and knife*
*Everything in sight*
*All locked down tight*
*Can't escape this city scene*

*Strangers here just passing through*
*Get city soul stuck on their shoe*
*Hurrying past these dark landscapes*
*Just some twisted, distorted shapes*
*Rising to the skies*
*Where all hope flies*
*Never landing in these streets*

It's not the same when it's just a game
Turn your back and there's no blame
Nothing feels right inside this city
The sky's just dark and the air's just gritty
No rainbow hues
Just dark city blues
Playing through the night

In nature time is carved in stone
But this city's heart is steel and bone
Lives spent herein constant trouble
Left behind in urban rubble
No pretty sounds
Just city sounds
Dark city blues tonight

# Night Shadow

There was a night when in the dark,
I sensed a shadow in my room,
A darker presence than the dark,
Lurking there within the gloom
At first it did not move at all -
Just darker black etched on my eye.
I started to reach out toward it;
But something told me not to try.

Within the silence of the night
I heard the faintest sound.
The shadow disappeared from sight
And was nowhere to be found.
Turning first this way then another
Seeking the darkness within the air
Reaching down I drew up my cover
To shield me from its stare.

It seemed forever had passed until
I dared pull the cover from my head.
A touch on my cheek became an icy chill
As it stood now beside my bed
My breath came rough and strangled
As the darkness drifted past
My covers newly tangled
Then onto the bed at last.

This night shadow sat upon my bed
Fear's cold weight sat there as well
My heart quickly filled with icy dread
That I'd never live to tell
Then this shadow in my night

*As silently as it had come*
*Faded slowly from my sight*
*With me left soaked and numb*
*As I tuned on every light*

*There are nights now I feel it near*
*That rustling sound within the night*
*As real as any other sound I hear.*
*But when on these nights I think I might*
*Look for this shadow spirit*
*Something warns me it would be quite*
*Safer to go nowhere near it.*

*Is this specter calling me?*
*If I look upon its face*
*What might be there to see?*
*And if I reach out to its embrace*
*Would it ever set me free?*

# Don T's Inferno

*Faded smiles*
*And countless miles*
*In nights that twist and turn*
*Years and years*
*Of sunburned tears*
*In days that sweat and burn.*
*Still it seems*
*It's only dreams*
*That spin and twirl*
*Within this world.*
*No signs to guide us*
*No guide beside us*
*We pass this way but once.*

# *Nighttime Labyrinth*

Black fades slowly into shades of greys
Colors follow on dim lit rays
A day begins that's not a day
Slowly pushing the dark away
Before me

Tonight I am young—only seven or eight
So, older thoughts will have to wait
Before me the land rises into the sky
Without a pause or question why
I start

Beyond the tracks of all the others
Floating there a bright cloud hovers
Waiting for me to find what's there
Perched above this valley air
It calls

Past slopes that tell me I must stop
With eyes set only on the top
I reach a point where the upward curve
Becomes so steep I lose my nerve
To go on

But I must find what's beyond that cloud
With its silent call that's so, so loud
So I once again begin to climb
I need to know just what I'll find
On the other side

On all fours I near the crest
Focused only on my youthful quest
I finally climb up past a ledge
And can see beyond the other edge

*Even past the sky*
*Into the wind I lean and stand*
*Before me lies another land*
*But it seems the same as I left behind*
*When I started on this long hard climb*
*To this place*

*Not exactly what I hoped to find*
*I sigh and search within my mind*
*What made me climb so high today?*
*To only end up where I may*
*Just as well not started*

*This ending is not what I'd planned*
*When I left behind my other land*
*But suddenly I feel a hand*
*And there beside me stands a man*
*Staring back at me*

*A siren shatters a moonlit night*
*Heart pounding I bolt upright*
*And briefly two worlds collide*
*Dark and light side by side*
*All is shattered*
*All that mattered*
*Seconds pass*
*I breathe at last*
*Then lay my head*
*Back on the bed*
*A slow exhale*
*And again set sail*
*The man that stared*
*No longer there*
*Was it my brother*
*Or just another*
*Face in my dream*

*Starting back down the hill*
*Windy fingers brush my hair*
*No reason to worry now*
*About someone who's nowhere*
*Halfway down I realize*
*I'm just not where I was before*
*Will my home still wait for me*
*There upon the valley floor*
*A voice from below calls my name*
*From what I hear it seems the same.*
*With my brother's voice to guide me*
*And his spirit here inside me*
*I smile.*

*Something wakes me from this dream*
*This time slowly—a slow-moving stream*
*Of waking thoughts emerge*
*But I resist and fight the surge*
*Of daytime thoughts and feelings.*
*Slowing my mind*
*I suddenly find*
*I'm back where I wanted to be*
*With the dreamscape there before me*
*But it's not the same sight*
*Nothing's quite right*
*So I pause and look around . . .*

*Feeling the sun warm my face*
*Deep within I find no trace*
*Of that other place*
*Now Time is changing*
*And I see I'm older*
*The wind is rougher*
*And the air is colder*

*A flash of light touches my eye*
*I walk upward and start to fly*
*Maybe something's different yet*
*I dare not stop or I'll forget*
*But another flash and I'm back in bed*
*Eyes watching sunlight slowly tread*
*Across my bedroom wall*
*Try as I might I can't go back*
*There's no path, no signs, no track*
*Confused emotions—nothing makes sense*
*In this nighttime labyrinth*

*I'm lost . . .*
*Lost in a dream*
*Where all rules change*
*And all exits seem*
*To just rearrange*
    *—my life.*
*Nothing seems quite real.*
*I don't know what to say*
*And I'm not sure how I feel*
*All I know is that today*
*I wake from yet another night*
*With no end of the dream in sight*

# The Huntress

*(To Kathryn 1)*

That night . . .
The moon called to me from within your eyes
Like purloined gold set in deep starry skies
As you moved closer I felt the fire in your soul
Burning white hot inside—barely under control
A beautiful sprite
Within the night
No mortal chains
Could ever hold
And . . .
Your tawny hair flashing highlights of gold
Beckoning all eyes to follow as catlike you strolled
Wrapped in sensuous sounds—the music of night
Came from inside you—clung to you tight
And in that sound
A sultry sway
Never found
Within the day
I was helpless—trapped by your stare
A smoldering look that singed the air
A beautiful huntress with eyes on her prey
My mind whispered run but my body screamed stay
Sensuous heat
I'd not felt before
Bound my feet
And barred the door
Then heaven's gate opened and the angels ran free
When the devil in you touched the devil in me

# *The Other Side*

*A poem of youth . . .*
*And growing older . . .*
*And learning to love again*

(To Kathryn 3)

When I was young, I watched the clouds
Drifting slowly through my skies.
I knew those windswept cotton shrouds
Hid so much from my eyes.

When I was young, I was convinced
That one bright summer day
There'd come a fairy prince
Who'd then lead me away
To another land . . .
    Where I would sail the sky in a great cloud ship
    And all below would seem like toys set upon the earth
    And I would laugh with the sun and moon.

So, I spent my youth with friends and games
And ice cream castles with candy canes
Within each day, burning bright
Each dream grew and then took flight
But jealous time without a sound
Whispered stories of what I'd find
If I'd set my feet on solid ground
And leave these childish dreams behind.

Time swept away my youthful skies.
And old winds stung my once young eyes.
Too late, I searched again to see
But was
    By cold winds tossed
    My way home lost
A door slammed shut behind me.

*I tried and tried to find my way back*
*Bright clouds now only grey*
*I stared and stared, but seemed to lack*
*The key to find my way.*
*No magic lived within my days*
*No magic in my night*
*No memory of my childhood ways*
*Could pierce the dull cold light.*

*Years adrift on a dreamless sea*
*No winds came to set me free*
*Until one day when Fate sent you*
*And slowly within me, something grew.*
*And one warm day we left the ground*
*Inside a jet and skyward bound*
*Soon cloud tops were lying far below*
*A mix of colors in the sun's pale glow*
*Something caught my eyes that day*
*Made me see beyond my window*
*Reflected there I saw the way*
*I could not find from down below.*

*In that reflection it all came back . . .*
*Within a flash—within your eyes*
*Familiar faces laughed with surprise.*
*Within those eyes of green and gold*
*A lifetime of stories waiting to be told*
*Because of you and our love shared*
*Because of you I once more cared*
*To see the magic that's born anew*
*Within each new day and within you.*

# Two Candles

*(To Kathryn 2)*

*Two Candles*
    *Within the Night*
*Swaying Softly*
    *Burning bright*
*Dancing Lovers*
    *Of fire and light*
*Lingering touches*
    *A flame ignites*

*Burning Beams*
    *Of love today*
*Chase cold Shadows*
    *Of doubt away*
*A beacon shining*
    *So, so bright*
*Within these candles*
    *Wrapped in this night*

# The Sea Inside Me . . .

# *Envy*

*Have you ever really watched a seagull fly*
*Floating there above the sky?*
*Have you ever really heard its laughing cry*
*And in that moment wondered why*
*We're stuck down here below?*

*And have you watched the dolphins leap*
*Playfully from the oceans deep*
*While we can only stand and keep*
*Dreams bound tightly in our sleep*
*That never let us go.*

# *The Sea Within Me*

*A black night sits on a blacker sea . . .*
*A dark-clad spirit reaching out for me*
*Far, far above—the stars still fly*
*Above these seas above this sky*
*Somehow the sea seems lonely here*
*Or perhaps it is just I.*
*And each tide calls*
*Before it falls*
*Melancholy songs*
*Of air and sea*
*I feel I belong*
*Within this song*
*Mirrored inside of me*

*The wind whispers softly past my ear*
*Hot breathy words I can't quite hear*
*Raising spirits from times now gone*
*When sailors sailed into each new dawn*
*And the tides did rise*
*Beneath the skies*
*And within each squall*
*A timeless call*
*For those who dare:*
*Heed and beware*
*Or just prepare*
*To stay*

*It seems so timeless within this sea*
*I feel so deep inside of me*
*And now . . .*
*A star slides down the black abyss*
*Igniting the sea with a gentle kiss*
*That burns wetly on my cheek*

# Voices in the Sea 1

A soft misty ocean blends into the sky.
Sea sounds echo a seagull's cry.
I stop and listen without knowing why,
Faintly hearing the sea song die.
And, as it ends I feel a chill
Brush by my soul . . . and I feel it still.
Something calls within me. I sense I belong
Within the realm of this ageless song.
Someone's gaze searches within me,
For a path, a gate, a door, a key.
Within this mist, within this glow
Within this sea and depths below
Within this wonder I've come to know
Within this madness that can scare one so
Within this still life of air and sea
Spirits wait to set me free.
The sea surface now a grey looking glass
Peering into a place time cannot pass.
Within these depths in deep-sea caves
Lie sailors bound in deep-sea graves.
A timeless sleep
Within this deep
And briny tomb below.

# Voices in the Sea 2

Within the deepest of the deepest seas
In a hurricane's fury along the Keys
Within the storm that devours the dune
Riding tides that race the moon
Within this dance of air and sea
Spirits wait to set me free.
Did sailors feel the same in times long past
Perched upon their midnight mast?
Thunder and lightning and briny foam
Each wave crashing its own way home.
Each moment weaving a tapestry
On a timeless canvas of air and sea.
Clouds racing by on phantom steeds
And sailors' bones within the weeds
That caught them long ago,
Holding them . . . still, caressing them so.
A timeless sleep
Within this deep
And briny tomb below.

# Caribbean Jewels

On top, the sea is spread with jewels,
Ephemeral gems in sunlit pools.
Riches for those that seek this wealth
Of sun and time and youth and health.
The sun burns white a sandy beach
While clouds sail by just out of reach.
Emerald seas dance under this sun
Chasing hungry birds that run
In and out of the sandy swash.

And by the sea in this lagoon
Lovers make love beneath each moon.
Within this sea so blue so bright
Within each steamy, balmy night
The soul of life has steeped so long
And made a brew so full, so strong
It sings to me a in a sensual song
And beckons me to stay.

For some, the call turns into obsession
And as they age, each barroom confession
Is retold with the past still brighter
And with days of sunlight so much lighter.
But the sea's song here is for the young
Then fades away like a song once sung.
Memories of nights with
    Wave sounds lapping
Against wooden ships
    with full sails flapping
Haunt their dreams.

*Within this sea is pure surrender*
*Within this sea is love so tender*
*Within this sea is a hazy sunrise*
*Set here for only lovers' eyes.*
*Within this sea are storms at night*
*Great rolling echoes of thunderous might*
*Laughing at those who feel cold fear*
*Crawling up the spiny thin veneer*
*Of their souls.*

*For this is a sea set in passionate climes*
*With spirits calling from more passionate times*
*No one can feel this summer heat*
*That touches soles of pretty bare feet*
*And leave it far behind.*

# *Colors of the Sea: Morning*

*Night fades slowly to a rosy dawn*
*Bleeding colors into a glowing sea*
*Last night's dreams too soon are gone*
*A new day's now breaking free*
*The air is moist—there is no wind*
*Glassy waves pause and then roll by*
*There's nowhere to go—no sails to trim*
*My spirits match this morning sky*

*If time were chasing I might regret*
*This morning here with no sails set*
*But for now it's good to move so slow*
*Under this muted morning glow*
*Yet morning colors are fragile hues*
*Pinks soon melt to subtle sapphire blues*
*Not far above—a lone cloud lingers*
*With morning hair streaked by sunlit fingers*
*A peaceful pace—nowhere else to be*
*Above this gentle morning sea*

*Then with the sun's first warm touch*
*Comes a tender reminder that such*
*Times cannot last forever*

*A breeze soon begins to rise*
*And now under these morning skies*
*Run rough-cut curls of white*
*While the skies turn midday bright*
*And the chameleon sea—now turquoise*
*Echoes all the chattering noise*
*From gulls and sea birds calling*
*Soaring high and falling*
*A circus of wings*
*While a mad chorus sings*
*The day begins*

# Sea of Sand

*Flying over a sea of sand*
*Carved and smoothed by unseen hands*
*The water that once knew it*
*As rivers coursed through it*
*Have abandoned this arid land*

*Across the ages*
*On windswept stages*
*March dunes of finest sand*
*White hot by day*
*At night they pray*
*To somehow understand*

# *On a Windward Beach*

An untamed wind blows from the sea
On a windward point—just you and me
Here the air's eternal breeze
Carves sharp-edged shapes
           on wind-pruned trees
The sun's hot touch on my bare skin
Ignites a fire that grows within
Everywhere sand
In this land
So dry

We hurry to the water's edge
Past the sand and past a ledge
Of coral set beside a pool
Into crystal water wet and cool
Her hot touch upon my bare skin
Fans the heat that burns within
A hot embrace
And our hearts race
Inside us

Everything's perfect in this place
No need to hurry—no need to race
Within the water and within me
The sun, the wind, the girl, the sea
And waves that push us to and fro
Helping passions grow and grow
The wind waking
Waves breaking
Inside us

# The Sound of One Man Laughing . . .

# I Fear Nothing

*I fear nothing—*
*Is not my battle cry*
*But a silent plea*
*That when I die*
*There will not be nothing there.*

# *Amid a Million Masks*

Amid a million masks
    I wear throughout the day
I have to pick each one
    From inside where they lay
Each a disguise
From prying eyes
But my real surprise
Is when I reprise
The same mask
    In a different way.

Amid my million masks
    I wonder what I see
Now no longer sure
    Which one is really me

# The Fairie World

*(For Ava and her dreams)*

The fairie world's a lot like ours
Except for all the fairie towers
Nestled there among the trees
And if you were to squint your eyes
And stare into the evening skies
As clouds ride on the sunset breeze
It might seem at first like home
But billowy sailing ships are known
To set sail just before dark
Each with a princess bright and young
Who softly sings the fairie songs sung
As they weigh anchor and embark
On their nightly voyage

Is that just a night bird calling?
With rising notes and sunlight falling
Far, far away within in the sky
I don't know but I've been told
That fairie ships are lined with gold
And leave golden streaks as they fly
Yes, their world's like our human land
Except for the night fairies in the sand
That pretend to just be crabs
But down below in their sandy homes
They feast on nectar
     and marshmallow scones
Covered with chocolate slabs
With elves and goblins and gnomes

*As the light begins now to fade
And dims into a twilight shade
Venturesome fairies here and there
Just might peek from under a flower
And look to see if now's the hour
To start walking in the air
Now, fairie children are just like you
Except they're small and can sleep in your shoe
And dressing like fireflies ride higher and higher
'Til they seem to just vanish into the night
But soon you'll see each star they light
When touched by their firefly fire*

*And beach fairies—they just love to play games
For sand in your shoes they're never blamed
Since you think it's just from the beach
Maybe if you turn your head just right
And pretend to look away—one might
Appear there just out of reach
Oh, if this were the fairie world
There inside that leaf that's furled
Might be a fairie queen
Yes, here between the sea and sand
If this were a magic fairie land
We could see those things unseen*

*So, the fairie world's a lot like ours
Except for all the fairie towers
Nestled there among the trees.*

# Tonight, Tonight Or Not

Part of me is still for footsteps listening
While our bodies intertwine
A sultry night with moist skin glistening
I need just a bit more time

Soft damp skin pressed so, so tight
Nothing left to get in the way
I've always dreamed of such a night
In dreams that taunt my day

Our bodies merge together
Our first time in this place
I want it to last forever
But passion sets our pace

I feel the urgency within the night
Now so hot it almost burns
But in the driveway a sudden light
Tells me her parents have returned

# Teenage Madness

To the girl whose name I thought I'd never forget
   To her whose name I now can't recollect

Night wraps around her.
Mystery surrounds her.
A lover, she talks.
A lioness, she stalks
A creature of night
Burning so, so bright.

I shut my eyes and still I find
Her image burning within my mind,
Like a memory that cannot die
Forever carved upon my eye.

Still, she haunts my nighttime dreams
And dances there in blue moonbeams
Moving to music only she can hear
So far away to be so near
So far away to be so near

# Greed

There are those who practice greed
Oh, please don't let us trouble you
The rest of us in times of need
Just love your new BMW.

These same people ask just what is wrong
In this world of violence and crimes
Between each prayer between each song
They preach family values of older times.

But in those older times I believe
People were more willing to share,
Not so ready to excuse their greed.
They tried harder to be fair.

Today it seems some get all the breaks
While others just get broken.
The takers, they seem to take and take
With every word that's spoken.

Sometime between now and then
We seem to have passed through a door
I don't know how or exactly when
They made a verb out of MORE.

They think others are just dumb
Never doing things that must get done
And in their world of black and white
Greed's their only Guiding Light.

*I guess I should turn my back*
*Walk away from those who only take*
*I feel sorry for the love they lack*
*And the pain left in their wake.*

*But, I know there'll come a time*
*When each stands at his heaven's gate*
*And above that gate will be a sign*
*We're sorry, we don't negotiate.*

# Tequila Wasteland

*Once upon a time I did not drink*
*Alcohol nor spirits—I did not think*
*It was right to confuse my mind*
*With whatever else I thought I might find*
*Inside my head*

*But one night I listened to what my heart said*
*There was nothing to fear inside my head*
*I could drink if I wanted and it would be fine*
*So maybe I should start with a big jug of wine*
*Just for fun.*

*I remember little about that night*
*Except the policeman blocking the light*
*As he stood above me with a serious frown*
*Telling me I had to turn the volume down*
*On my stereo*

*For a while that cured me of my quest*
*To find for me the very best*
*Spirits that could call my name*
*And take me where I was not the same*
*As I was before*

*But then I discovered there was definitely more*
*Bourbon and rum and vodka to pour*
*Lots of friends and lots of fun*
*From cool midnight breezes to hot noontime sun*
*We lived*

Tropical beaches with a painkiller drink
Sailboats heeling almost to the brink
Dancing late to steel drum bands
Making love in warm wet sands
By moonlit seas

Only one wrong turn in all that time
When I first found tequila and a lime
Life was so sweet with the tequila taste and
I found myself in a Tequila Wasteland
With salt on the rim.

## If Truth Were a River

*Lowering her voice she looked into my eyes*
*Words so sincere there could be no lies*
*Our magic she said would last forever*
*In dreams we'd sow and nurture together*

*The night was humid and oh so hot and*
*Memories like this are never forgotten*
*Her husky voice said that I'd be her first*
*Well, if truth were a river I'd have died of thirst*

# Southern Tea

The lady standing at my front door
Was vibrant still at ninety-four
With an embossed card passed to me
I'd just been invited to a Southern Tea
The following afternoon

Her piercing eyes of crystal blue
Looked at me and saw right through
My blossoming excuses died on the vine
And I heard a voice trying not to whine
Say—Yes, I'd love to go

Now summer in Vicksburg's awfully hot
And I'm the type that sweats a lot
So as I stared in my closet at clothes
I tried to make sure that whatever I chose
Wouldn't look too bad wet

The morning of the Tea was true to form
Hazy blue sky—humid and warm
And as the day drifted on toward four
More heat marched in on a victory tour
And it wasn't over yet

A chorus of insects had plenty to say
Basking in the heat of that long day
But at the time appointed I had to go
And dragging my feet ever so slow
I walked up to her front door

She answered the door in a diaphanous gown
And in her hair was a beautiful crown
Of summer flowers so bold and bright
I had to smile at this amazing sight
As she walked me to her yard

*As she led me back to her formal table*
*I didn't know if I'd be able*
*In this heat to drink much tea*
*But when asked if she could pour for me*
*Of course I just said yes*

*Past the teacups and past the tea*
*Out from hiding came her own Southern Tea*
*The moment she started I knew for a fact*
*What she was pouring was straight Black Jack*
*Into an oversized glass*

*When asked if I wanted ice in my drink*
*Expecting some mixer I couldn't think*
*So then she added with a playful frown*
*I agree—ice only waters it down*
*And she handed me my Tea*

*Once before when a guest in her home*
*I'd seen a picture—a girl standing alone*
*As I was captivated by this beauty before me*
*The lady said softly that the girl was she*
*When she was only twenty-one*

*And today she seemed twenty-one again*
*As she sipped and flirted with all the men*
*And as I drank more of the Southern Tea*
*I learned that she could still outdrink me*
*The hard way*

# The Dove and the Pigeon

My young ears were filled with Bible stories told
Of demons, of angels and temples of gold
At first—every song on every nun's tongue
Sounded even holier than the last song sung
Old Testament tales of sand and sandals
And graven images lit by blazing candles
God-fearing vengeance between each tribe
Begot holy wars—so hard to survive
Warrior angels armed with spears of spite
Winds and floods gave proof to God's might
But made no sense at all

Then—New Testament tales of giving and love
A God as gentle as the gentlest white dove
Who actually loved all people the same
Regardless of what their God was named
A new God who didn't need to fight
To show his strength and prove his might
Soon churches were formed to spread his word
But strangely it wasn't the message I'd heard
Somehow the dove turned into a warrior pigeon
Well if God made man then man made religion.

# *Meandering*

*Time meanders*
*At no set pace*
*A careless clock with a*
*Pale blank face*

*Start in the middle*
*Move to the ends*
*A complex riddle*
*Of twists and bends*

*Sometimes too fast*
*Sometimes too slow*
*So much is past*
*So far to go*

*Thinner and fatter*
*Fatter and skinnier*
*Doesn't matter*
*Time's not linear*

# Epilogue:

# Dreams Never End

*Now we slip away from daylit skies*
*And dreams are writ upon our eyes*
*By playful muses marking time*
*Within our nighttime sleeping mind*
*In these tales of their design*
*On paths unmarked we follow blind*
*And on these roads of twists and bends*
*We never seem to reach an end*
*Passing through worlds and worlds again*
*As one story ends another begins*
*No rush to finish no race to win*
*It's seem to me that dreams never end*

www.ingramcontent.com/pod-product-compliance
Lightning Source LLC
Chambersburg PA
CBHW020124130526
44591CB00032B/519